First World War
and Army of Occupation
War Diary
France, Belgium and Germany

60 DIVISION
Divisional Troops
Divisional Signal Company
4 October 1915 - 31 December 1915

WO95/3028/4

The Naval & Military Press Ltd
www.nmarchive.com
Published in association with The National Archives

Published by

The Naval & Military Press Ltd

Unit 10 Ridgewood Industrial Park,

Uckfield, East Sussex,

TN22 5QE England

Tel: +44 (0) 1825 749494

www.naval-military-press.com

www.nmarchive.com

This diary has been reprinted in facsimile from the original. Any imperfections are inevitably reproduced and the quality may fall short of modern type and cartographic standards.

© **Crown Copyright**
Images reproduced by permission of The National Archives, London, England, 2015.

Contents

Document type	Place/Title	Date From	Date To
Heading	WO95/3028/4		
War Diary	Bishops Stortford	04/10/1915	24/11/1915
Heading	War Diary Of 60th (Lon) Divnl Signal Co RE From 1st December 15 To 31st December 15 Vol No.1		
War Diary	Bishops Stortford	01/12/1915	31/12/1915

WO 95/30284

Army Form C. 2118

WAR DIARY
or
INTELLIGENCE SUMMARY
(Erase heading not required.)

Instructions regarding War Diaries and Intelligence Summaries are contained in F. S. Regs., Part II. and the Staff Manual respectively. Title Pages will be prepared in manuscript.

1/1th SIGNAL COY,
1st LONDON DIV. ENGINEERS.

Place	Date	Hour	Summary of Events and Information	Remarks and references to Appendices
Bishops Stortford	Oct. 4		TRAINING.	
			3 officers and 3 men attend a Farriery Class, Bishops Stortford.	
	" 5		3rd Army tactical scheme. Company bivouac at Newton Hall, Dunmow.	
	" 6		ditto. do. at Black Notley.	
	" 7		ditto. do. at Newton Hall, Dunmow.	
	" 8		Returned to Bishops Stortford.	
	" 12		1 man attached to Saddlery Class, Technical Institute, Bishops Stortford.	
	" 13		Artillery tactical exercise for officers only.	
	" 14		12 men attached for instruction in Magneto Exchange working.	
	" 17		Application made by 181st Brigade for 2 motor-cyclists; application not granted.	
	" 19		Divisional Manoeuvres. Company are billeted at Dunmow.	
	" 20		do. do. at Tirling.	
	" 21		do. do. at Dunmow.	
	" 22		do. returned to Bishops Stortford.	
	" 28		12 men attached for instruction in Magneto Exchange working.	

1875 Wt. W593/826 1,000,000 4/15 J.B.C. & A. A.D.S.S./Forms/C. 2118.

Army Form C. 2118

WAR DIARY
or
INTELLIGENCE SUMMARY

(Erase heading not required.)

SIGNAL COY,
LONDON DIV. ENGR......

Instructions regarding War Diaries and Intelligence Summaries are contained in F. S. Regs., Part II. and the Staff Manual respectively. Title Pages will be prepared in manuscript.

Place	Date	Hour	Summary of Events and Information	Remarks and references to Appendices
Bishops Stortford	Oct.11		**EQUIPMENT.**	
	"		3 motor cycles received, completing establishment.	
			CHANGES IN STRENGTH.	
	Oct.9		Total strength = 7 officers, 214 other ranks.	
	" 11		2/Lieut. Pook, W.G., proceeded overseas.	
	" 12		2/Lieut. Williams, C.C.H., proceeded overseas.	
	" 18		1 man to Home Service Battalion.	
	" 19		1 N.C.O. and 4 Dvrs. attached to replace those sent to Transport School, Shoreham.	
	" 28		1 man to Home Service Battalion.	
			Sgt. A.E. Thresher gazetted 2nd Lieut.	
			Total strength = 6 officers, 212 other ranks.	
			REMOUNTS.	
	Oct.25		Inspection by Col. Long. 2 horses cast.	
	" 26		7 horses sent to Veterinary Hospital.	
	" 31		1 horse received from Veterinary Hospital.	
			Total strength = 99; deficiency of 8.	
			GENERAL	
	Oct.4		Lieut. R.J. Poynton buried.	
	" 13		Zeppelin seen at 8 p.m. steering southward; Headqtrs. advised by telephone.	

Army Form C. 2118

WAR DIARY
or
INTELLIGENCE SUMMARY

SIGNAL COY,
LONDON DIVL. ENGINEERS.

(Erase heading not required.)

Instructions regarding War Diaries and Intelligence Summaries are contained in F. S. Regs., Part II. and the Staff Manual respectively. Title Pages will be prepared in manuscript.

Place	Date	Hour	Summary of Events and Information	Remarks and references to Appendices
Bishops Stortford	Oct.15		GENERAL (Ctd.)	
			Request received from Central Force for officer willing to serve overseas with East Anglian Signal Coy. None willing.	
	" 16.		Medical inspection at 12 noon.	
	" 28.		Cpl. Leach met with motor cycle accident at Stark Hill; found unconscious at 8 p.m.	

Army Form C. 2118

WAR DIARY
or
INTELLIGENCE SUMMARY

(Erase heading not required.)

Instructions regarding War Diaries and Intelligence Summaries are contained in F. S. Regs., Part II. and the Staff Manual respectively. Title Pages will be prepared in manuscript.

Place	Date	Hour	Summary of Events and Information	Remarks and references to Appendices
Bishops Stortford	Nov. 1		**TRAINING.**	
			Telephone Instructional Course in Magneto Exchange Working at Old Post Office - 12 men attached.	R.
	23	Noon	3rd Army Training scheme.	R.
	23	"	Commenced work at Saracen's Head, Dunmow. 3 Cable Wagons proceed to Stebbing, Felsted and Little Waltham.	
	"	2 p.m.	Arrived Stebbing.	
	"	2.30	Arrived Felsted.	
	"	2.54	Arrived Little Waltham.	
	"	5 p.m.	Communication interrupted on all lines.	
	"	7.8	Communication restored with Stebbing.	
	"	6.58	Communication restored with Felsted.	
	"	6.20	" " Little Waltham.	
	"	8.30	Office closed. Company billet at Great Dunmow.	R.
	Nov.24	7 a.m.	Office opened.	
	"	10 "	Office closed at Great Dunmow: Company return to permanent quarters at Bps. Stortford.	
	"	12.30	Company arrive at Bishops Stortford.	R.
	"	p.m.		
	Nov.25	2 p.m.	Entraining scheme at Bishops Stortford Railway Station.	
	"	5.30	Return to Grange Stud Farm Stables.	
	"		Telephone Instructional Class in Magneto Exchange Working at Old P.O. - 12 men attached.	R.
			CHANGES IN STRENGTH.	
			Total strength - 8 Offrs 210 Other Ranks	V.
	Nov. 2		1 recruit joins from Administrative Centre.	V.
	" 3		ditto.	V.

Army Form C. 2118

WAR DIARY
or
INTELLIGENCE SUMMARY

(*Erase heading not required.*)

Instructions regarding War Diaries and Intelligence Summaries are contained in F.S. Regs., Part II. and the Staff Manual respectively. Title Pages will be prepared in manuscript.

Place	Date	Hour	Summary of Events and Information	Remarks and references to Appendices
			CHANGES IN STRENGTH - Ctd.	
	Nov. 6		Cpl. Palmer, A.S., discharged as physically unfit for war service.	
	"		1 man medically unfit for foreign service proceeds to join Home Service Details.	
	Nov. 8		1 recruit joins from Administrative Depot.	
	Nov.10		1 man medically unfit for foreign service proceeds to Home Service Details.	
	Nov.14		ditto.	
			Total strength - 8 officers; 210 other ranks.	
			REMOUNTS.	
	Nov. 5		2 horses proceed to Veterinary Hospital, St. Albans.	
	" 19		1 horse transferred to A.S.C.	
	" 22		1 horse received from Veterinary Hospital.	
	" 23		2 horses received from 2/24th Batt.	
			Total strength - 98.	
			GENERAL.	
	Nov. 1		Sgt. Woodhouse, B.W., gazetted II/Lieutenant.	
	" 4		No. 3 Brigade Section proceed to Braintree, attached to 181st Inf. Bde.	
	" 7		Application received from Bandsman Kirwin for transfer to this Coy.; referred to 3rd Line Rating Board.	
	" 8		Conference of O.C. Brigades and Divl. Troops, Drill Hall, Bps. Stortford, on matters of discipline and interior economy.	

Army Form C. 2118

WAR DIARY
or
INTELLIGENCE SUMMARY

(Erase heading not required.)

Instructions regarding War Diaries and Intelligence Summaries are contained in F.S. Regs., Part II. and the Staff Manual respectively. Title Pages will be prepared in manuscript.

Place	Date	Hour	Summary of Events and Information	Remarks and references to Appendices
	Nov.14		GENERAL – Ctd.	
			Enquiry from O. i/c. Supplies re disposal of manures; unsaleable.	
	" 15		Rating Board.	
	" 18		Inspection of billets by G.O.C.	
	" 24		O. i/c. Supplies to dispose of manure at 1/-. per load.	

Captain
Ldn. Signal Coy. R.E.

Confidential

War Diary of

60th (Lon) Divl. Signal Co. R.E.

From :- 1st December 15
To :- 31st December 15

Vol: No. 1

Army Form C. 2118

WAR DIARY
or
INTELLIGENCE SUMMARY
(Erase heading not required.)

Instructions regarding War Diaries and Intelligence Summaries are contained in F.S. Regs., Part II. and the Staff Manual respectively. Title Pages will be prepared in manuscript.

Place	Date	Hour	Summary of Events and Information	Remarks and references to Appendices
BISHOPS STORTFORD	1/12/15		Extract from III Army Orders prohibiting the photographing or sketching of any part of the coast etc. or any military works etc. intimation of formation. Published in Company Orders.	EL
		9.30. 11 a.m.	Training to R.C.O.s on apparatus and power jointing on cable. Lecture to II Lt. Hawthorne (WOODHOUSE)	
		11 a.m. 10 p.m.	Cable drill - Line Telegraphists under Lt. ANDREWES	
"	2/12/15		Result of examinations in sending and receiving on Buzzer, and Elementary Electricity. For testing Field Line Telegraphists announced. Four men in no. 2 Section and 1 man in No. 1 Section qualified for the higher rating.	EL
	3/12/15		The first of the men are inspected by his Orderly Officer at 7 a.m. parade	EL
	4/12/15		45 men of R.C.O.s proceeded on Week-end leave after duty at 12.30 p.m.	
About	4/12/15 4.00 p.m.		No. 76 Gpl. MORRIS, H. Snd. met with accident in riding - Removed to Clearing Hospital ELSENHAM by order of A.D.M.S.	EL

WAR DIARY
or
INTELLIGENCE SUMMARY

(Erase heading not required.)

Army Form C. 2118

Place	Date	Hour	Summary of Events and Information	Remarks and references to Appendices
BISHOPS STORTFORD	5/12/15	9.30 a.m.	Church Parade to Divine Service at BIRCHANGER Church.	EA
	6/12/15	10.30 a.m.	Court of Enquiry to enquire into accident to motor cycles assembled at Signal Office. President: Major W.S. MULVEY 3/3rd East. Riding Field Coy. Members: Lt. E. ANDREWES 60th East. Riding Signal Coy., 2nd Lt. A.O. BROWN 2/1st Northern Field Coy.	
			No. 2172 Pnr. GOLDSMITH H.A commenced attendances at Armourers Course of Saddling at Technical Institute BPS. STORTFORD this day.	SA.
	7/12/15	9.45a.m - 12.30p.m.	Office telephonists carried out "Traffic" scheme at GRANGE STUD FARM under II Lt. GENT (GRIST). Results very satisfactory as to speed of sending & accuracy, with few exceptions. A good knowledge of the message form & office routine shown generally. Own to low illegibility regular practice in sending & receiving in begun.	EA
	8/12/15	5.00 p.m.	Cable-laying practice by night. R detachment laid cable from Signal Office BISHOPS STORTFORD to MANUDEN - 3½ miles - in 2 hr. 30 min. SR detacht. to MUCH HADHAM - 5½ miles in 3 hr. 45 min.	EA

WAR DIARY or INTELLIGENCE SUMMARY

Army Form C. 2118

Place	Date	Hour	Summary of Events and Information	Remarks and references to Appendices
BPS- STORTFORD	8/12/15		Batt: training & night [tactical?] L detail. to LITTLE HADHAM - 3 miles in 1 hr. 30 min.	
		10 a.m.	Court of Enquiry on accident to Pte. Gilbert (see entry 7/12/15) re-assembled to hear evidence of M.O.	
			Extract from Batt. Reg. Orders No. 266. 7/12/15 (published in Company Orders this day) "It is notified for information that no N.C.O. or man is permitted to be on licensed premises except between the hours of 4 p.m. and 9 p.m."	
			"Out of Bounds." "The King of Prussia" public house SAWBRIDGEWORTH HERTS, is placed out of bounds to all members of H.M. Forces from 5th Dec. '15.	EC
"	9/12/15	7 a.m.	Firemen road along lines and farmers sight at dawn. Signals good in all trucks.	
		11 a.m.	O.C. Coy. inspected billets - applied to have BARRELL'S DOWN RD. added to billeting area.	
		6½ p.m.	Lt. WHITEMAN left B.P.S. STORTFORD for M. tem to dental treatment.	EC

Army Form C. 2118

WAR DIARY
or
INTELLIGENCE SUMMARY

(Erase heading not required.)

Instructions regarding War Diaries and Intelligence Summaries are contained in F. S. Regs., Part II. and the Staff Manual respectively. Title Pages will be prepared in manuscript.

Place	Date	Hour	Summary of Events and Information	Remarks and references to Appendices
BPS - STARTMPD	10/12/15	10 a.m.	Court of Enquiry to enquire into loss of equipment at Old Port Office attempted. President: Major MULVEY. 3/3rd Lbn. Field Cy. Members: Lt. E. ANDREWES. 60th Lbn. Signal Cy. 2 Lt. B.F. NELL. 1/6 th. Lbn. Field Cy.	
			Training. Riding acm. country for mounted staff.	2a.
	11/12/15	10.30 a.m.	9 R.C. Os and 86 men proceeded on trek and train.	2b.
	12/12/15	9.30 a.m.	Church Parade for church service at BIRCHANGER CHURCH	2c.
			Letter received by O.C. Sig. Cy. from O.C. No. 3 Section complaining of lack of equipment for telephone signalling. As brigade to which he is attached is now short of complete brigade with definite duties of home defence attached to it, represented that issue of adequate equipment is most urgent. The supply of this equipment is now urged by O.C. Sig Cy. Letter in "Investigation" file.	2d.

1875 Wt. W593/826 1,000,000 4/15 J.B.C. & A. A.D.S.S./Forms/C. 2118.

WAR DIARY
or
INTELLIGENCE SUMMARY

(Erase heading not required.)

Army Form C. 2118

Place	Date	Hour	Summary of Events and Information	Remarks and references to Appendices
B.P.S. STORTFORD	13/12/15	5 p.m.	Capt. Training. Cable - laying practice by night. SR detail. OAK HALL & YEW TREE INN MANUDEN miles. Time.	
			RL " " to LITTLE HADHAM miles. Time	
			SL " " " MUCH HADHAM " "	
	14/12/15		Capt. SLADEN 2nd i/c as member of District Court Martial 179 & Inf. Bde.	
		3.15 p.m.	By Instructions received in letter from the C.R.E. Inspector OGDEN inspected the Transport of this Company on behalf of the G.E.R. No property of the Railway Company was found in possession of the Signal Company.	
			Postal Arrangements. Extract from Divl. Eng. Orders No. 269 10/12/15. Coy. Orders "Instituting the practice of delivering private correspondence to Billets. No. 211. 11/12/15. Published in Company Orders for no such commencing 11/12/15. All correspondence to be addressed No. -- Rank -- Name -- Unit -- Town	

Army Form C. 2118

WAR DIARY
or
INTELLIGENCE SUMMARY
(Erase heading not required.)

Instructions regarding War Diaries and Intelligence Summaries are contained in F. S. Regs., Part II. and the Staff Manual respectively. Title Pages will be prepared in manuscript.

Place	Date	Hour	Summary of Events and Information	Remarks and references to Appendices
BPS. STORT-FORD	15/12/15	9.45 a.m. to 4.30 p.m.	Training. Cable detmts. laying cable from SR from LITTLE HADHAM to GREEN TYE. " " " " GRANGE STUD FARM to LITTLE HADHAM. " " " " LITTLE HADHAM to BRAUGHING. Cable reel'd up Portsmouth returned to GRANGE STUD FARM. 4.15 to 4.30 p.m.	Ll. App. A Pt. II Orders Orders 214 attached A do. B do. C Lt.
	16/12/15	10 a.m.	Board of Enquiry to check stores attempted at Signal Office. Transfers. R.C.O's & men transferred between returns of to-day. Appears in Coy. Orders this day. Unnecessary tonnage by Tpoph. (Extract from 60th (Kdn) Divn. Orders No. 349 13/12/15.) Memorandum in Coy. Orders this day.	Lt.
	17/12/15	10.6 p.m.	Cable detmts. SR & SL laid cable from H.Q. 179th Bde BISHOPS STORTFORD to Acting Father MIDFORD for England. Bi'ple'scheme. Lt. WHITEMAN reported reported for duty. Arrangement not in post. re giving out escort orders of air raid H.Q.O. telephone runt of this division. SR & L Cable detmts. reel'd up & train cont. yesterday.	Lt. Lt.

1875. Wt. W593/826 1,000,000 4/15 .I.B.C. & A. A.D.S.S./Forms/C. 2118.

Army Form C. 2118

WAR DIARY
or
INTELLIGENCE SUMMARY

(Erase heading not required.)

Instructions regarding War Diaries and Intelligence Summaries are contained in F.S. Regs., Part II. and the Staff Manual respectively. Title Pages will be prepared in manuscript.

Place	Date	Hour	Summary of Events and Information	Remarks and references to Appendices
BPS STORT-FORD	18/10/15		43rd R.E. Oz. proceeded on trek and Ewrs after shoots ad and eng. Transferring H.T. Co. & men between sections in accordance with Coy Orders 21a (15/12/15) att. Chn. of Charles at 9.30 a.m. for divine service at "BIRCHANGER" church	Ea.
"	19/10/15			Ea.
"	20/10/15	9.30 am	Inspection of Manchester Or. C. Sections. Inspection of Riveter by M.O.	Ea.
"	21/10/15		Capt SLADEN proceeds on leave till Sunday next; Lt. E. ANDREWES assumed command of the company. Giving instruction & drivers by Sgt. Maj. MARRIOT A.S.C. Mounted officers riding & jumping.	Ea.
"	22/10/15	1 p.m.	BRIG.GENL ROPER (3rd Army) (60th Div) accompanied by the C.R.E. inspected the company Stables at "GRANGE STUD FARM." GENL ROPER remarked on the horses and being finished with manger. Capts Sections approved.	Ea.
"	23/10/15		Sewing & drivers and cart drill for cattle sections.	Ea.
"	24/10/15	9 a.m.	Company paraded at 9 a.m. for inspection by G.O.C. 60th Div, at 9.30 a.m. in MAPLE AVENUE. Inspection moved & G.O.C. in column of route. The G.O.C. remarked on the importance of transport signalling by Finish. Own form of signalling of this Signal Coy. standard to the state in	Ea.

WAR DIARY or INTELLIGENCE SUMMARY.

Army Form C. 2118.

(Erase heading not required.)

Instructions regarding War Diaries and Intelligence Summaries are contained in F.S. Regs., Part II. and the Staff Manual respectively. Title pages will be prepared in manuscript.

Place	Date	Hour	Summary of Events and Information	Remarks and references to Appendices
BISHOPS STORTFORD	25/12/15	9.30 a.m.	The company paraded at 9.30 a.m. for Church Parade at "BIRCHANGER" Church.	J.A.
do.	26/12/15	7 a.m.	Special order by G.O.C. 60th Div. conveying gracious message of H.M. The King for Christmas day was read out in T.A.M. Parade. [dated 24/12/15]	
		11 a.m.	Meeting of Officers of Divisional Engineers (60th Div.) at C.R.E's Office. The C.R.E. conveyed to the Officers the criticism of the G.O.C. 60th Div. after inspection of the Divisional Engineer Units on 24th inst. He urged O.C. Companies to make every effort to get all deficiencies in equipment and clothing made good. He suggested that inspections parades should be held m.a. week in all companies. Capt. A.G.L. SLADEN returned from term of absence.	J.A.
do.	27/12/15		This day observed as holiday.	Fortnight musketry by G.O.C. 60th Div. dated 24/12/15
		10 a.m.	Company competitions in Despatch Riding, Cable Laying, & staving pace started at "WICKHAM HALL" Farm.	
		5.30 p.m.	Company at dinner at "GRANGE STUD FARM". Being competition after at "WICKHAM HALL" Farm.	J.A.
do.	28/12/15	3.5 p.m.	12 R.E.O's from R.T.Q. & R.E.D. Units of The 60th Div. reported at the Signal Office to attend course of instruction in Cable Laying and Telephone Signalling.	J.A.

2353 Wt. W2544/1454 700,000 5/15 D. D. & L. A.D.S.S./Forms/C. 2118.

Army Form C. 2118.

WAR DIARY
or
INTELLIGENCE SUMMARY.
(Erase heading not required.)

Instructions regarding War Diaries and Intelligence Summaries are contained in F. S. Regs., Part II. and the Staff Manual respectively. Title pages will be prepared in manuscript.

Place	Date	Hour	Summary of Events and Information	Remarks and references to Appendices
BISHOPS STORTFORD	29/10/15	9.30 a.m.	Course of instruction for N.C.O.s of R.T.B. — R.G.A. commenced at "GRANGE" STUB FARM under Lt. WOODHOUSE. Section training.	—
do.	30/10/15		Section training.	—
do.	31/10/15		Section training.	—